How To Gain
Victory
Over Memory Loss

Live Your Life In Victory

How To Gain Victory Over Memory Loss

Pastor Jason Alvarez
The Love of Jesus Family Church, Pastor

Jason Alvarez Publishing

PASTOR JASON ALVAREZ

How To Gain Victory Over Memory Loss
Copyright © 2012 by Jason Alvarez

ISBN 13: 978-0615689999 (paperback)
ISBN-10: 061568999X

Published by Jason Alvarez Publishing
448 Highland Ave
Orange, NJ 07018
(973) 676-4200
www.theloveofjesus.org

Unless otherwise indicated, all Scripture quotations are taken from the King James Version of the Bible.

Special thanks to Sonya Kimble-Ellis for her assistance with the editing of this book. Sonya's work has appeared in magazines, newspapers, and online news sites. She is the author of several books for children and teens.

Also, a special thanks to Naimah Ward, Owner & Founder of FirstFruits Publications & Productions for assisting with the editing and publishing of this book.

All rights reserved. This publication is protected under the copyright laws of the United States of America. Except for appropriate use in works of scholarship and reviews, reproduction or use of this work by Internet or any other electronic, mechanical, or other means, including photocopying and recording, and in any information retrieval system, or any other form, is prohibited without the express written permission of the author.

TABLE OF CONTENTS

1   Introduction: The Call Into Ministry   7

2   The Battle Begins: My First Battle With Memory Loss   12

3   Principles And Weapons Of Power   17
       Don't Cast Your Pearls Before Swine
       Truths & Nuggets of Wisdom to Live By
       The Cause
       The Weapon of Confession
       Exercising Your Mind
       Prayer of Thanksgiving

4   Prayer Is Your Key   35
       My Private Prayer Life
       Acknowledgement Prayer

5   Prevailing Prayers For The Church   42

Preface

This is not a medical book. *"How To Gain Victory Over Memory Loss"* is a book of TRIUMPH for those who have been experiencing memory loss! It is a testimony of a miracle healing I received from the Lord that contains powerful principles, nuggets of truth and life changing prayers that every believer should know in order to be victorious and successful in their life's journey.

There are so many amazing truths in this book and I believe just one of them will change the course of your life forever! You will learn how you can gain victory over a problem that affects many people.

A Must for Every Believer!

Chapter One

INTRODUCTION: THE CALL INTO MINISTRY

Let me share with you how I was called into the Pastoral Ministry. I was in New York City with my wife who was ministering in a small Church there. All of the sudden, I heard a Voice asking me, "Jason, do you love me?" With that Voice came this overwhelming presence that caused me to begin to silently weep and lose sight of everything and everyone else in the room. I gently answered, "Yes Lord, You know that I love You." Then the Voice said, "Feed my sheep!" Again, He asked me, "Jason, do you love me?" Again I answered, "Yes Lord, You know that I love You." He said, "Feed my sheep!" Then, that Voice asked me the third time, "Jason, do you love Me more than these?" And again I answered weeping, "Yes Lord, You know that I love You." He said unto me, "Feed My lambs!" By this time, I was no longer weeping silently. I was beginning to weep uncontrollably. Honestly, I didn't understand all that was happening to me at the time. All I knew was that I was having a *"God Moment"* that I would treasure for the rest of my life. Amazingly, my life went on for a while as if nothing had happened that night. Then, all of a sudden, a Holy desire to Pastor began to invade and influence every area of my life. Somehow on the inside of me, I knew that I was called to Pastor God's precious people but yet nobody else believed that I was called to Pastor. They all believed that I was called to be an Evangelist. *NEVERTHELESS*, you couldn't beat it out of me with a baseball bat! I kept telling them I know, that I know, that I know, that I am called to be a Pastor. They just laughed and thought I was nuts but no matter what anyone else thought about it, I just couldn't shake it off. It just so happened that around this time, I was traveling with Evangelist R.W. Shambach, doing a tent revival in Los Angeles. I preached in the day service and did Praise and Worship in the night services. Well, a Pastor from that area asked me to minister at his church and so I ministered that Sunday night and God manifested himself greatly to my utter surprise. *To God be all the glory*! After the service, the Pastor asked me, "What do you sense God is calling you to do with your life young man?" So I said to him, "I believe God has called me to Pastor but no one believes me. They all believe that I'm called to be an Evangelist." Then he said to me, "Young man, I am going to be praying for you. I'm going to talk to God about you tonight!" Well, I'd heard that before and honestly those words meant nothing to me. Why? Because many times I had said those same words to others and the truth of the matter is that I never prayed for them. I never even remembered their names. So I went to the hotel room that night and had a good night's sleep. The next morning a young man picked me up and took me to the airport. As I was ready to board the plane, I heard someone calling out my name from afar. I turned around to see who it was and to my amazement I saw the Pastor from the night before running through the airport like O.J. Simpson! He was trying to get to me before I boarded the plane. Well, I stepped out of the line and ran to meet him because to be honest with you, I didn't know what was going on. All I knew was that he was all out of breath and sweating profusely. Despite that, the first thing that Pastor did was give me a big old hug. Then he said to me, "I've been praying for you all night young man. God spoke to me and told me to tell you YES, He has called you to Pastor and as you begin pastoring one of the very unique things that you'll see happen is that you will begin to grow right along with the people. The Lord also told me to tell you that you will eventually reach the world with the Gospel of Jesus Christ from that church." *And I believed him.* He then said, "Go home and start your church! Go home and start pastoring, for the Lord has surely called you!" WOW! I couldn't believe it. This Pastor had really prayed for me like he said he would and God answered him and confirmed my Call through him. What a God! See, there are still people out there that are God sent, men and women whom God will use to supernaturally — help and bless us. This Pastor became one of the most instrumental people in my Christian life and I hardly knew him; yet God in His love and wisdom divinely orchestrated the whole thing and placed him in my life just at the right time. Do you know that I never saw or heard from that Pastor again? I believe this was a *"God connection,"* a Kairos moment; a space in time where God put all the pieces together all by Himself. There was nothing missing, nothing lacking. Well, here is the gospel truth - not long after that, I started a Church called The Love of Jesus Church in Orange, New Jersey. Today, 25 years later, I'm still pastoring that wonderful Church which is literally impacting millions around the world!

TO GOD BE ALL THE GLORY!

I have learned by experience. FAITHFUL IS HE THAT'S PROMISED, WHO ALSO WILL DO IT!!!

Chapter Two

THE BATTLE BEGINS: MY FIRST BATTLE WITH MEMORY LOSS

My first battle with memory loss began in a supermarket. I can remember it as if it was today. Some things in life just have a way of leaving a vivid lasting impression. This experience in particular was carved deep into my spirit so that it would never be forgotten. I was at Kings Supermarket shopping for my wife when I suddenly heard a voice say, "The reason you're beginning to forget things is because at your age, it's natural for one to begin to experience memory loss." I had just turned forty-five years old. I remember that voice saying that memory loss was normal. It was something to be expected. But quite frankly, I wasn't expecting it at all. Yet, it still came. Why? It's because the storms of life always come uninvited and unexpected. This is why you have to always be on your guard and stay ready. Well, needless to say, the battle was ON! Immediately, I rebuked it. I knew it was a lying spirit that was looking for a foothold in my life. It was using the old lie concerning memory loss that multitudes have already fallen prey to. Suddenly, I remembered the Lord once telling me, "Son, the reason the devil has had such great success in so many people's life is because he has succeeded in training and deceiving man to defeat himself." For example, here was a lying spirit attempting to deceive me with a lie that says when you reach a certain age, it is normal for you to start experiencing memory loss. What a LIE! Yet so many people have fallen prey to it. I have actually heard people laugh when talking to others about it. They say, "See, you must be getting old. Your memory is beginning to fail." They laugh about it. How dumb is that? Well, I don't think that's funny and I'm not going to sign for that bill of goods and neither should you! Memory loss is a very serious thing and it's nothing to laugh about. I honestly thought that this spirit of memory loss that had begun to affect me would just leave with one good rebuke. But little did I know that it would not go away without a major fight. Suddenly, I found myself finding it difficult to remember such things as the names of individuals or the names of certain things or places. Man, it was a major battle! So I began to fight back as best I knew how, but to no avail, this thing was getting the best of me and I knew it. I was suddenly struggling in areas of my life that at one time were no struggle for me at all. Of course, I didn't let anyone know what I was dealing with, for I strongly believed that it would soon go away and everything would just go back to normal. *But boy was I wrong!* It just kept getting worse and worse. With it also came that tormenting voice of fear attempting to literally paralyze me. It relentlessly tempted me to believe and accept the worst. It kept telling me that in time I would not even be able to remember my own name. Can you believe it? I tell you, if you let it, fear will put you in an early grave! It will torment you until you can't even think straight. This is why I believe fear is man's number one enemy and if not dealt with at the onset, it will gradually grow and grow until it literally breaks you down and eventually destroys you! You see, through personal experience, I have discovered that when fear tries to grip you, and you do nothing about it, it will intensify and just get bigger and bigger, and bolder and bolder. It's true. Fear must be resisted at the onset in Jesus Name, or fear, which is a spirit with a personality, will literally weaken your knees and totally mess up your mind. This is why I thank God for *2 Timothy 1:7, For God has not giving us the spirit of fear, but of power, love, and of a sound mind (KJV)*.

Now here are two things that are vital for you to know. First, fear is a spirit and Jesus Christ has given us power over ALL the power of the enemy. That simply means that I can speak to it in the Mighty Name of Jesus and fear will have to go! Secondly, God has not given me the spirit of fear! Therefore, I don't have to receive it! And on top of that, I don't want anything operating in my life that doesn't come from my Heavenly Father. How about you? Well, I must admit, that during this trying time (2 Timothy 1:7) became my battle ax and weapon of war. I found myself using it continuously. You might ask, "Did it help?" The truth is that it helped some, but not totally. Although it kept me in the fight and did not allow the enemy to fully prevail, I still found myself struggling greatly and not gaining the kind of ground I had anticipated. But thank God I was determined to persevere no matter what. For deep down on the inside of me, I knew that in time God would bring me out. Although I must admit, I didn't know how or when, I just knew He would and thank God, eventually He did. The truth of the matter is that some battles just take longer than others to win! But again, I was determined that no matter how long it took, I was not going to go down in defeat!

Why? Because deep down on the inside of me I knew that eventually God would turn things around for me if I didn't quit! Did you hear that? I said I knew that eventually God would turn things around for me if I didn't quit! Now here is where most people lose the battle:

1.) They give up many times without a fight and accept memory loss as the will of God. DON'T YOU DO THAT!

2.) They quit too early. Winston Churchill said, "NEVER, NEVER, NEVER QUIT!" I say Amen! You see, I have discovered that it will always take the hammer of persistence to drive in the nail of success because VICTORY never comes easy, BUT IF YOU PERSEVERE, YOU WILL PREVAIL!

Well, I was determined to never quit and because I didn't quit, God eventually gave me the victory over memory loss. The good news is that if He did it for me, He will do it for you because He's no respecter of persons. With that being said, in the next chapter, I want to provide you with some of the keys, that I learned to put into practice during this challenging time in my life. These are the principles that helped me gain victory over memory loss and I believe they will help you do the same. Now you must apply these principles on a daily basis. You can't slack off. Remember, this is a great battle that you're in and it will require all of you - not just some of you!

Chapter Three

PRINCIPLES AND WEAPONS OF POWER

Don't Cast Your Pearls Before Swine

While you are battling to overcome memory loss, you have to make sure that you don't share your battle (memory loss) with individuals that don't have your best interest at heart. If you do, instead of helping your situation, you may wind up sabotaging your good efforts. Are you aware that most individuals innocently share their problems with those who do not really care enough about them to pray for them or put the secrets of their heart into a vault of loving protection? Rather, they use it for gossip, casting pearls before swine, or revealing your secrets to others just to make themselves look good. How sad! I have learned by experience that when people gossip about you, it releases the spirit of witchcraft to work against you. This is why Isaiah 54:17 is so powerful and should be in every believer's arsenal and daily life. I use it on a daily basis and so should you.

Isaiah 54:17 *"No weapon formed against you shall prosper, and every tongue which rises against you in judgment you shall condemn. This is the heritage of the servants of the Lord, and their righteousness is from Me says the Lord."* (New King James Version)

Let me give you an example. Every day I BOLDLY confess or say out loud, "NO WEAPON THAT IS FORMED AGAINST ME SHALL PROSPER, AND EVERY TONGUE. . ." (Notice the words

And every tongue! And every tongue!) Why does it say "*And every tongue that shall rise up against you in judgment*"? I'll tell you why! It's because if the devil can get people to speak against you through gossip, a judgmental spirit, or through bitterness and hate, then he can unleash the spirit of witchcraft against you. This is why it is so important that you daily hold up this scripture as a shield of faith and weapon of war. Because you don't know what's being unleashed against you through the mouth of others. Look at these amazing scriptures!

Proverbs 12:18

"There is that speaketh like the piercings of a sword: but the tongue of the wise is health."

(New International version) *"Reckless words pierce like a sword, but the tongue of the wise brings healing."*

Psalm 55:21

"The words of his mouth were smoother than butter, but war was in his heart: his words were softer than oil, yet were they drawn swords."

(New Living Translation) *"His words are as smooth as butter, but in his heart is war. His words are as soothing as lotion, but underneath are daggers."*

WOW! And so every day, I boldly confess:

"No weapon that is formed against me or my family shall prosper, and every tongue that shall rise up against us in judgment, I condemn! I say you're brought to naught! I say you're rendered helpless and are of no affect to work against us in Jesus' Name. I say you're proven to be in the wrong and your assignment against us is cancelled in Jesus' Name. For this is the heritage of the servants of the Lord, and their righteousness is of me, sayeth the Lord of hosts."

Then I confess Job 5:12-14:

Satan it is written and now on record. God frustrates and disappoints your devices, so that your hands cannot perform their enterprises against us in the name of Jesus. I say you meet with darkness in the day time and you grope in the noon day as in the night time, and all your plans and all your strategies are of none affect to work against us in any way, form or fashion, in Jesus' Name."

Again, these are just a couple of good scriptures for you to put to memory and use on a daily basis. And when you pray these prayers (Isaiah 54:17 and Job 5:12-14) on a daily basis, don't forget to put your loved ones' names in there as well.

Truths & Nuggets of Wisdom to Live By

To start with, *never say something you do not want to believe.* Why? It's because you are the most believable person in your life. This is why our *confession of faith* is so powerful. Are you aware that you will believe what you say before you believe what anyone else says?

Secondly, *never say something you want others to forget and something you do not want others to repeat.* Why? The reason is because the power of life and death is in the tongue. Notice that I didn't say that life and death is in the devil's power, but in the power of the tongue and I don't want people breathing life into things that should die in my life, or should just stay dead. Nevertheless, I'm fully persuaded that the greater the battle, the greater the victory; the greater the test, the greater the testimony. I believe it! I also believe that you do not qualify for anything you're not wiling to fight for. Benson Idahosa once said to me, "A man should never complain of failure if he has never made an all out attempt to succeed." Now that's a mouth full!

I am fully persuaded that the key to every good ending is, YOU STAY WITH IT UNTIL YOU WIN! For example, in Psalm 78:9-41, you'll find some of the saddest scriptures in the Bible. Listen to this. *"The Children of Ephraim, being armed and carrying bows, turned back in the day of battle."* Psalm 78:41 says: *Yea, they turned back, and tempted God, and Limited the Holy One of Israel.* Can you believe that? I'm literally blown away by those scriptures. The Bible says that if we turn back in the day of battle, we will limit Almighty God. WOW! The one thing you do not want to do is limit God! And one of the ways you limit God is by quitting before the battle ever starts or quitting right in the middle of a battle. I know by first hand experience that sometimes things can get extremely rough; but if you don't quit, in time, God will turn it around for you and you will experience great victory in Jesus' Name. This is why Galatians 6:9 tells us *"So let's not get tired of doing what is good. At just the right time we will reap a harvest of blessing if we don't give up."* (New Living Translation)

This one thing is for sure: Defeat is always bitter, but on the other hand, victory is oh, so sweet! This is why your healing for memory loss is so much worth fighting for. DON'T QUIT! DON'T EVEN THINK ABOUT IT! DON'T GIVE IN! DON'T EVEN THINK ABOUT IT. REMEMBER, WINNERS NEVER QUIT AND QUITTERS NEVER WIN! Hear me! I strongly believe that God is going to see you through this dark time in your life and give you a great victory, just like He did me. Yes, I am fully persuaded. God is going to turn it around for you. Just watch and see. Don't you quit! Remember, this is an exceeding, great, and precious promise of God and He is watching over His Word ready to make it good in your life! And He will make it good! Yes! He will bring you through in Jesus' name!

The Cause

Here is something I recently discovered or that came to me by revelation. Because I often pray in the spirit, my mind or intellect was not being exercised as much as it should have been and as a result, my memory began to pay the price for it. But thank God for my Helper and Teacher the Holy Spirit, who in a flash or in a moment's time, began to speak to me from I Corinthians 14:14: *"For if I pray in an unknown tongue, my spirit prayeth, but my understanding is unfruitful."* The Amplified Bible says it this way – *"For if I pray in an [unknown] tongue, my spirit [by the Holy Spirit within me] prays, but my mind is unproductive [it bears no fruit and helps nobody]."* So from this scripture I began to clearly understand that there is a big difference between me praying with my intellect or my understanding and me praying in the spirit by the help of the Holy Spirit. When I pray in my known language, I am praying with my intellect or my understanding. On the other hand, when I pray in the Spirit, my mind is unproductive because it is my spirit that's praying by the help of the Holy Spirit within me. And so, praying in the Spirit bypasses my mind or intellect and reaches down into the reservoir of my spirit, which is unlimited, being tied to God and by faith, I utter words energized by the Spirit but not known to the intellect. I think that's awesome, don't you?

Now here is another amazing revelation! Are you aware that praying in the spirit is like having a personal direct hot line to the throne of Almighty God? Wow! I love it. Romans 8:27 says when I pray in the spirit, the Holy Spirit himself helps me to pray or make intercession for the saints according to the perfect will of God. Man, is that good or what? Have you ever felt that you needed to pray for a friend or a loved one, but you just didn't know what to pray for because you didn't know what he or she needed or was going through? All you knew was that they needed prayer. Well, when we pray in the spirit, the Holy Spirit knows exactly what they need. So when I yield myself to Him in prayer, He begins to give me divine utterance to pray according to the perfect will of God for that individual. In doing so, I bypass my intellect, which may be totally in the dark. The result is that I'm making intercession for my friends or loved ones, according to the perfect will of God. You can't miss. Oh thank God for the Holy Ghost, our Great Helper!

Another great benefit about praying in the spirit is that after you have prayed a while; your mind eventually gets quiet before the Lord. And in doing so, it allows you to be able to hear from God more clearly, without your mind interfering or getting in the way through fear, anxiety, or worry. Now that's absolutely the truth. But in my case, it was beginning to work against me because I was not exercising my mind and memory enough. And again, thank God for the Holy Ghost, for He did not leave me in the dark. He began to pour revelation knowledge into my spirit through His Word, and boy, am I ever grateful!

Now here is where I found the MASTER KEY to help turn things around for me. When I realized I was not exercising my mind or memory enough, I knew I had found the ROOT CAUSE. Now, I could work on the CURE. You see, your mind or your memory is like a muscle. The more you use it, the stronger it gets. The less you use it, the weaker it gets just like anything else. In a flash, it dawned on me that I need to develop an exercise routine for my mind and memory, just like I have one for my physical body. This way, my memory can become fruitful, strong and productive again. WOW! I SAW IT! I COULD TASTE IT! I knew I had received the master key that would soon unlock my victory. This is why it is so important to have balance in every area of your life! I also discovered that when it seemed that I could not remember certain things, I could literally ask the Holy Spirit to BRING TO MY REMEMBRANCE THE THINGS MY MEMORY HAD FORGOTTEN AND TO MY AMAZEMENT HE BEGAN TO DO SO. Try it! The next time you need something brought back to your memory that you seem to have forgotten, ask the Holy Spirit to help you and watch what happens. Now remember! In order for you to gain victory over memory loss, YOU MUST EXERCISE YOUR

MEMORY BY PUTTING A DEMAND ON IT. So when you ask the Holy Spirit to bring something to your remembrance that you seem to have forgotten, and it doesn't happen in 20 or 30 seconds. Don't Give up. Stay with it until the Holy Spirit pulls it up. And Trust me. He Will!

Here's another great truth! In Romans 8:26, we read these amazing words, *"...the Spirit also HELPETH..."* Oh, how those words lift and greatly encourage me knowing I'm not alone in this. It greatly blesses me. Again, the Spirit also HELPETH our infirmities, weaknesses or inabilities simply tells us that if we have need of His assistance, just ask Him and He will help you! Are you aware that what Jesus was to the twelve when He was here on earth the Holy Spirit is that to us now? Oh thank God for our Helper, the wonderful person of the Holy Spirit!

Here's another nugget of truth!

John 14:26, Jesus said, *"But the Comforter (Counselor, Helper, Intercessor, Advocate, Strengthener, Standby), the Holy Spirit, Whom the Father will send in My name [in my place, to represent Me and act on My behalf], He will teach you all things. He will cause you to RECALL (will REMIND you of and bring to your REMEMBRANCE) everything I have told you."* (Amplified version)

Wow! Did you get that? He will cause you to RECALL, (will REMIND you of, and bring to your REMEMBRANCE) everything I have told you. Wow! Wow! Wow! Do you need His help? Start asking Him for it. HE'S WAITING ON YOU!

1.) To help you to recall
2.) To remind you of
3.) To bring to your remembrance everything you need

GLORY TO JESUS!

Weapon of Confession

Another weapon that I have used to overcome memory loss is the weapon of confession. For example, Proverbs 10:7 states that, *"The memory of the just is blessed..."*

So I boldly confess:

"My memory is blessed and not cursed for I am the righteousness of God in Christ. I have a sound mind and the Holy Spirit brings all things to my remembrance in Jesus' Name. It is written that I can do all things through Christ who daily infuses me with inner strength! I boldly confess that I do not forget; not even one of your benefits

Father for you forgive all my iniquities. You heal all my diseases. You redeem my life from destruction. You crown me with tender mercies and loving kindness. You satisfy my mouth with good things, so that my youth is renewed like the eagles. You teach me to profit and lead me in the best paths for my life. My cup is running over and my heart is filled with praise at the mention of Your name. I thank you Heavenly Father. My memory is blessed and not cursed, in Jesus' Mighty Name."

I strongly encourage you to use these scriptures daily to fight against the loss of your memory. Many don't really believe in the power of confession. But I do. Especially when I read scriptures like Jeremiah 1:12 where God tells us, He's watching over his Word, ready to perform it and make it good in our lives. How amazing is that? So apply His Word daily and continuously as a battle axe and weapon of war, and watch the enemy flee in terror in Jesus name!

Exercising Your Mind

In I Thessalonians 1:2-3, Paul said, *"We give thanks to God always for you all, making mention of you in our prayers; Remembering without ceasing your work of faith, and labour of love and patience of hope in our Lord Jesus Christ, in the sight of God and our Father"*. The word 'remembering' literally means to exercise your memory. Wow! This is exactly what God showed me. He said that in order for you to get victory over memory loss you will have to discipline yourself daily to exercise your memory just like you discipline yourself daily to exercise your physical body.

Let me remind you what Jesus said in John 10:10,

"The thief cometh not, but for to steal, kill, and destroy, but I am come, that you might have life, and have it more abundantly or till it overflows."

Listen! Having memory loss, is not having abundant life. So let me encourage you to REBUKE the devil in Jesus' Name and GET UP! Don't lie down and give up! Get up again and fight back! The Bible says, Stand, and after having done all, stand. So stand your ground in Jesus' Name! For victory is yours! Victory is on the way! Again, I encourage you not to give up, but to do the simple things that are in this book on a daily basis and watch God perform a miracle in your life. See, the beautiful thing is that I have created prayer slots that require both my intellect and memory to be exercised on a daily basis. These are prayers based on the Word of God. You can start with 5 or 10 minute exercises or 15 or 20 minute exercises. It's all up to you. You don't have to use my prayer outline. If you desire, you can make and use your own. The master key is that you must begin putting a demand on both your intellect and memory on a daily basis. This must be done if you are going to experience healing for memory loss. Again, I'm not just talking about you reading a book to stimulate your mind. No, I'm talking about making a daily demand on your mind to recollect information already stored in your memory on a daily basis.

Today I can joyfully report to you that now my mind and memory is not just sound and strong, but is sharper than it's ever been. Now on the other hand, the truth is that there are still days when I have to fight my way through and put the very things that are in this book to practice on a daily basis, over and over again. And so the battle is never over, but the victory is always promised if we will persevere and not give up. Remember that if God did it for me, He'll do it for you; for God is no respecter of persons! And the master key is that you must put a demand on both your intellect and memory on a daily basis if you are going to experience healing for memory loss.

Prayer of Thanksgiving

This Prayer was born out of Romans 1:8 where the Apostle Paul prayed: *"First, I thank my God..."* I call this prayer *"The Prayer of Putting First Things First."* The psalmist wrote, "I will enter His gates with thanksgiving in my heart. I will enter his courts with praise." So let's begin...

Heavenly Father, I come to You in the precious and matchless name of Your son Jesus Christ, my Savior and Redeemer. Today, I want to say thank you Heavenly Father for Your tender mercies and loving kindness. Thank you for Your grace and Your embrace, Your warmth, Your corrections, Your reproof, Your instructions in righteousness. Thank you for Your keeping power. I thank you today Heavenly Father for keeping me as the apple of Your eye, safe and sound from harm, dangers, accidents, freakish things and vandalism. Today, I want to say thank you for being my Dad; for loving me the way You do. Thank you for never ever giving up on me Heavenly Father. I know that if it had not been for You, I would have never made it this far. So I want to say thank you precious Heavenly Father. Amen!

Today, I want to say thank you for being my Present Help in times of trouble. Thank you for being my Shelter from the storm, my High Strong Tower and my Hiding Place. Oh Abba Father, hide me in the secret of Your presence from the pride of man. Keep me secretly in Your pavilion from the strife of tongues and lead me in Your way, in Jesus' Name. Father, today, all that is within me blesses your Holy Name. Heart bless the Lord; stomach bless the Lord; lungs bless the Lord; emotions bless the Lord; memory bless the Lord. Let all that is within me bless Your Holy Name. I boldly confess, my mind is alert and my heart is receptive. Father, I do not forget any of Your benefits. For You forgive all my iniquities. You heal all my diseases. You redeem my life from destruction. You crown me with tender mercies and loving kindness. You satisfy my mouth with good things so that my youth is renewed like the eagle. When I walk, I won't get weary. When I run, I will not faint, for the Lord is the strength of my life and my portion forever and ever. Amen!

Today Heavenly Father, I want to say thank you for Jesus Your wonderful son, my Savior and lover of my soul. Oh Jesus, thank you for being my Lord and my Savior, my Healer, my Redeemer, my Rock and my High Strong Tower.

*I want to say thank you Lord Jesus for your unfailing, your unending, your undying, self sacrificial love Lord. Today, I thank you for your Word oh God. For it is written, Christ has redeemed me from the curse of the broken law by becoming a curse for me. For it is written, cursed is every man that hangs on a tree, so that the blessing of Abraham might come upon Jason Alvarez (*put your own name here*) through Jesus Christ, that I might receive the promise of the Spirit through faith as a result of Your shed blood on Calvary. Jesus, I boldly confess that Abraham's blessings are mine. They're mine! They're mine! They're mine! Therefore, I boldly confess that I am blessed coming in and I am blessed going out, I am blessed in the city and I'm blessed in the field. Whatsoever I set my hands to, I thank you Heavenly Father that You cause it to flourish, prosper, and succeed at my hands. Thank you for making me the head and not* *the tail. Thank you for putting me above only and never beneath. Thank you for causing me to ride upon the high places of the earth. Thank you for crowning me with Your favor as with a shield and covering me with a coat of many colors. I thank you Lord Jesus for blanketing me with Your love from the top of my head to the soles of my feet. I boldly confess, I cannot be defeated and I refuse to quit. I've been redeemed by the blood of Jesus. I've been washed from all my sins and as a result, I've been made a king and a priest unto God my Father through Your shed blood. Oh King of Kings and Lord of Lords, I praise Your Most High name. For you have been given a name above all other names, and at the sound of Your name, every knee must bow and every tongue must confess that You are Lord and Master to the Glory of God the Father. Today, my Lord and my Savior, I want to say thank you from the bottom of my heart for saving me, keeping me, and for bringing me this far. I will forever be grateful. Lord Jesus, today I want to say thank you for the precious Holy Spirit.*

Holy Spirit, I want to say thank you for Your Person, Presence, and Power in my life. Thank you for being my Comforter and Counselor. Thank you for being my Helper, my Guide, my Intercessor, my Strengthener, my Standby and my Lawyer. Thank you for being my all in all precious Dove of Heaven. Today I want to say thank you for choosing to love me and to live in me forever and ever. Thank you for standing by me when all others have forsaken me. I'm so humbled by the fact that You, who know me best, love me most, and I don't ever have to fear being myself with You. For You know my uprising and my down sitting. You know my thoughts afar off. Before I even utter a word, You already know what I'm going to say. Oh Holy Spirit, I'm so glad You're in my life. Help me to treasure Your Presence, Your love, and your friendship. I don't know what I would ever do without you. Holy Spirit, there's no one that can compare with you. Today Holy Spirit, I ask You to inspire me, enlighten me, empower me, energize me, and electrify me with your Glorious Power to do the works of Jesus and even greater works. Teach me to love like Him, to have compassion like Him, to be merciful like Him, to please the Father like Him. I need You Precious Holy Spirit. I need You every moment of every hour of every day. Draw me closer than ever before to the heart of the Father. Help me to see Jesus in all His Glory and Splendor. Give me a deeper revelation of Your precious Word and grant me Holy boldness to speak your Word without shame, fear or compromise in Jesus' Name, AMEN.

So today, I want to say thank you Heavenly Father for being my Dad. Thank you Lord Jesus for being my Savior and my Soon Coming King. Thank you Holy Spirit for being my sweet Friend and Comforter in Jesus' Name, Amen!

Chapter Four

PRAYER IS YOUR KEY

My Private Prayer Life

Another prayer that I use to exercise my mind is called the *prayer of acknowledgement*. On top of using this prayer to combat memory loss, I also have learned to use it to keep God involved in every area and aspect of my personal life. I will let you in on a little secret. For many, many years, it appeared as if I had the golden touch. It seemed that whatever I did had God's divine approval on it. My rod constantly blossomed and I was successful in every endeavor of life. Well, at this time in my life, I was praying daily the specific prayer that I'm about to share with you. But then, for some strange reason, I suddenly stopped praying that prayer. Personally, I believe that *pride* just got a hold of me. Somehow, I thought that all the success I was experiencing was all my doing. It was my wisdom, my charisma, and my strong personality. What a joke! Well, the consequences were devastating and for a couple of years, my life became a constant struggle. Man, was I miserable. Although I learned much during those tough years, I was never able to connect the dots. I just never realized how much impact that *little* prayer had made in my life. It was as if there was an invisible umbilical cord tying God's heart to mine. Little did I know that through that simple prayer, God had been feeding and directing me every step of the way. So once I stopped praying that prayer, it was as if the umbilical cord that had been feeding and directing me all that time was severed. As a result, I stopped getting divine direction from God on my every day affairs. What a tragedy! Well, thank God that's all behind me now.

However, I'm going to share with you what happened. One day, years later, as I was walking and praying as I do every day, the Holy Spirit gently spoke to me and once again reminded me about the *prayer of acknowledgment* and its importance in my life.

That simple but profound prayer is found in Proverbs 3:6:

"In all thy ways acknowledge Him and he shall direct thy paths."

Take notice of the first six words. In all, not some, but IN ALL THY WAYS ACKNOWLEDGE HIM! Now I'm not talking about acknowledging Him with every little detail of life, like when I am getting ready to cross the street or getting ready to have a cup of coffee. For those things, I just use common sense and personal preference. Now let's get back to my story! So once again, I began to pray this prayer, covering every major part of my life on a daily basis. Without exaggeration, in a couple of months, things began to drastically turn around. The first thing that happened was that God's voice started to become crystal clear again and I began to receive divine direction for my life. I always say that everything meaningful in life begins with divine direction or what the Bible calls a gift of the Word of Wisdom! Oh yes, without divine direction, you're like a chicken without a head; ever moving, but not knowing where you're going which reminds me of a story from many years ago that happened to me when I traveled with the great Evangelist Nicky

Cruz. One beautiful summer night, we headed out to a meeting that was about an hour away. So after an hour and a half passed, I asked the driver, "Do you know where you're going?" He answered me with broken English, "No man, but God does." Well, he kept driving and driving and we kept getting further and further away from our desired destination. So after another half hour, I asked him again, "Hey man, do you know where you're going?" He answered me once again, "No man. But God does!" So finally I just said to him, "Listen man, if you don't know where you're going, but God does, why don't you just ask him to show you?!!" That's my point altogether. If you don't know where you're going and God does, why don't you just ask him to show you?! Well, it was a huge thing for me to begin to receive divine direction for my life again. For up to that point, I felt as if I was just drifting away, or just existing. Yet another major thing happened to me right after that. I came to the place where I made a deal with the Holy Ghost that once again changed things drastically in my life. Would you like to know what that deal was? I said, "Holy Spirit" from this day forward, let's make a deal. You lead and I'll follow. Just show me the way!" Wow!!! That has turned out to be the best deal I've ever made and yes, the Holy Spirit has taken the lead once again. As a result, things have taken a 180-degree turn in my life for the better. Glory to God!

So, the *prayer of acknowledgement* actually became a two edged Sword for me. It allowed God to be involved in my daily life again;

and in months, I began to experience great success. It also helped me develop a prayer routine, where my memory was being exercised daily and as a result, I broke the back of the enemy, and gained the victory I so desperately needed over memory loss. So remember, I want to remind you that the key to the healing of memory loss is to develop a daily exercise routine for your mind and memory, just like you have one for your physical body.

Today, I encourage you to do the same and develop your own memory exercise routine, so that your mind and memory can once again become fruitful, strong and productive. Now just as I do, you may want to add your own present needs, wants and desires to these prayers once you learn them. Or, you can continue to use the prayers in this book if you so desire. Remember, this is just a simple pattern for you to get started on your own prayer life. The important thing is for you to put these prayers to memory and pray them every day until you are able to memorize them and eventually begin adding your own words, needs, and desires to them. Now let's get started!

Prayer of Acknowledgement

Heavenly Father, I come to you in the precious name of thy Holy Son Jesus, my Lord, my Savior and soon coming King. You said in Your Word, in all your ways acknowledge me and I will direct your paths,

I will make straight paths for your feet. Today, I acknowledge You with my life, my wife's life, my children, and in the lives of my children's children, believing You to direct my paths in Jesus' Name. I acknowledge today with my future and with LOJ's (The Love of Jesus) future, believing You to direct my path. (LOJ is the name of the church I Pastor. You can put the name of your own church) *I acknowledge You today Heavenly Father with my staff, believing you to direct my steps. I acknowledge You today with every place I go to minister outside of LOJ ministries, from France on down. I acknowledge You with the monies in the bank and the investments for LOJ ministries and my own life, believing You to direct my paths. I acknowledge You today with the vacations I'll take the rest of this year, believing You to direct my paths in Jesus' Name. Heavenly Father, I acknowledge You today with our Saturday morning missions' outreach. I acknowledge you with the food pantry ministries, the world wide missions' outreach, and the door-to-door evangelism, believing You to direct my paths. Precious Heavenly Father, I acknowledge You with the empty lots in Orange, believing You to direct my paths. I also acknowledge You with the rental properties, believing You to direct my paths. Father, today in Jesus' mighty Name, I acknowledge You with our Sunday services and our special Sunday night guest speakers, believing You to direct my paths. I acknowledge You today, oh God, with the sale of the mall, believing You to direct my paths, in Jesus' name. I believe I receive the mall sold quickly, in Jesus' Name and I shall have it!*

Today, Heavenly Father, I acknowledge You with the old works, the new works and the works that will be started in the future, believing You to direct my paths, in Jesus' Name. I acknowledge You with the West Orange property, believing You to direct my paths. I acknowledge You with our World Outreach Missions department, believing you to direct my paths...

So on and so forth. I will do this concerning anything that concerns me, and even future things that I am thinking about doing. I do this sometimes a month to a year in advance. I tell you, it is vital that you understand this simple but critical principle. In all your ways, not some, but in all your ways acknowledge or recognize Him. Never forget, He should never be an after thought!!! He said, in all your ways acknowledge Him and He will, not maybe, not hope so, but He WILL direct or make straight paths for your feet.

Now if you don't want to hit and miss, do what He said! In all your ways acknowledge Him, and He will direct your paths. I have shared one of the greatest secrets I know of for success. Now, it's up to you! Do this exercise everyday without fail. Then, watch how you begin to experience the miracle of healing for your memory loss. Remember, expectation is vital! What is expectation? I say it this way: I've got my neck stretched as far as it will go, looking over the fence of impossibilities, into the land of miracles, where I belong. I expect miracles every day in Jesus' name and so should you.

Chapter Five

PREVAILING PRAYERS FOR THE CHURCH

In conclusion, here are some of the prayers that I have committed to memory and pray daily for the church that I Pastor. These prayers not only help me exercise my memory, but they also produce amazing results for my church and personal life. Now, since I am a Pastor, I pray these prayers for the church that I oversee; but, even if you aren't a Pastor, you can pray these prayers for the church that you attend.

Prevailing Prayers for the Church

"Heavenly Father, I lift up LOJ (Put the name of your church here) *before You in the Name of Jesus. I lift up every aspect and every respect of LOJ in Jesus' Name. I pray for the Word of the Lord to have free course and be glorified here at LOJ in the Name of Jesus. I pray for my brothers and sisters to be delivered from unreasonable and wicked men for all men have not faith. Today, I pray for the Word of the living God to grow and multiply mightily at LOJ and throughout this entire area, in Jesus' Name. I pray for a great number of city officials, school teachers, school principals, entrepreneurs, business men and women, CEO's of great companies, blue collar workers, white collar workers, police men and women, firemen, professional athletes, professional entertainers, doctors, lawyers, architects, engineers, property owners, contractors, builders, backsliding preachers, and intercessors, backsliding musicians and singers, computer operators, computer technicians, and computer geniuses to*

become obedient to the faith at LOJ Ministries where I pastor in the name of Jesus. I pray Heavenly Father that you will plant their roots deep in the soil of Your house at LOJ in Jesus' Name. May they become trees of righteousness that you may be glorified. I believe You for it and I praise You by faith in advance in Jesus' Name. Today, I lift up before you every man and woman, every young person who is ordained to eternal life that lives in the Oranges, Newark, Irvington, Bloomfield, Glen Ridge, Verona, the Caldwells, Montclair, Maplewood, Millburn, and Union, in the name of Jesus. I claim their salvation in Jesus' Name and their deliverance out from under the power of the devil to the power of the risen Christ. Today, I step out into the realm of the spirit and I come against you, you spirit of Islam in the name of Jesus. I bind you and break your power over the lives of these people, in Jesus' Name. I come against you, you spirit of witchcraft and antichrist, you foul religious spirit, you spirit of new age and atheism. I break your power over these individuals in Jesus' Name from the least to the greatest, from the youngest to the oldest. I cancel your assignment against them and render you totally powerless to work against them any longer in Jesus' mighty name. Heavenly Father, I ask You to open the heart of every person in this entire area, just like you opened the heart of Lydia to receive Jesus Christ as Savior and serve Him with Honor as Lord, all the days of their lives in Jesus' Name. Right now, I loose the spirit of grace and supplication. I loose the spirit of prayer and intercession. I loose the spirit of travail upon LOJ and its people, in Jesus' Name. Heavenly Father, I pray that You will enlighten and empower Your people to travail in prayer until multitudes are birthed into the kingdom of God, in Jesus' Name. I pray for men and women who at one time in their lives were born again, but for some reason or another, they fell away. I pray that You will enlighten and empower Your people to travail in prayer until Christ is formed in them again and they are restored to full fellowship with you Heavenly Father, in Jesus' Name. Precious Heavenly Father, I ask You in Jesus' Name to send prosperity upon LOJ and its precious people. Set before our people an open door that no man can shut, in Jesus' Name. Set before our people an open door for them to have jobs and better jobs, and even great jobs in Jesus' Name. I pray Heavenly Father that You will set before our people an open door for business opportunities; for inheritances to be loosed upon our people in Jesus' Name; and for monies owed and monies tied up in court cases to be released into the hands of our people now, in Jesus' Name. I boldly confess that my God liberally supplies and fills to the full every need I have according to His riches in glory by Christ Jesus. I boldly confess that I believe I receive a hundred times as much as I have sown in the past three years to come back to me before this year is over, in Jesus' Name. I boldly confess that I believe I receive the wealth of the wicked being transferred and place into my hands for whom it's been laid up as the righteousness of God in Christ. I loose large checks and large donations to come into my hands and into the hands of LOJ before this year is over, in Jesus' Name. I prophesy money cometh to me in Jesus' Name. From every sphere of life and every corner of the earth I prophesy abundance and not lack will be in my life. I prophesy fatted calves and not skinny goats are my portion. I prophesy that I always have enough, and yea, more than enough. For El Shaddai, the God who is more than enough provides for me. I come against every hindrance that will try to hinder any of these things from coming to pass. I command you, be thou removed, and be thou cast into the sea, in Jesus' Name. Now Angels of God, I commission You to go forth and prosper my way before me, and cause these things to come to pass in my life to the Glory of God in Jesus' Name. Today, I roll all my works upon the Lord. I commit and trust them fully into Your hands Lord, believing You to cause my thoughts to come into full agreement with Your will, so that my plans will be established and succeed, in Jesus' Name. Amen. So be it!"

These are some of the prayers that I use on a daily basis, that have helped me to overcome memory loss and to greatly prosper in every area of my life. I have committed these prayers to memory and have disciplined myself to pray them even when I don't feel like it. Your mind is a muscle and it must be exercised just like any other part of your body. Many individuals experience memory loss because they do not exercise their mind and memory on a daily basis. Therefore, if you are going to win the battle over memory loss, you are going to have to exercise your mind every day, and put the simple principles that are in this book to practice continuously. Again, these prayers are just some of the prayers that I use. You can use them until you develop your own prayer exercise routine. The important thing is to get started today. Don't wait until tomorrow! My friend says it this way, "Don't join the tomorrow club, start right now!" Don't let the devil lie to you any longer. You are not losing your mind. Perhaps, you just haven't been exercising your memory like you should. But now, things are going to change!

Remember, I am not trying to teach you something that I got out of a book, or what someone else told me. This is a testimony of my real life experience in battling memory loss. All I know is that God delivered me, but I fought for it, tooth and toe nail. And only through the grace of God, was I able to win the battle. If God did it for me, He will do it for you, for He is no respecter of persons. Now, Go Forth in Jesus' Name and win your battle over memory loss!

I KNOW YOU CAN! AND I BELIEVE YOU WILL!

Pastors Jason & Gale Alvarez

The Love of Jesus Family Church 15 years ago... Entering into our 26th year! To God Be All The Glory!

PASTOR JASON ALVAREZ CDS & TEACHING SERIES

Title of Powerful Teaching Series	Price
Attitudes	$20.00
A Study in Brokenness	$30.00
Cycle of Faith	$20.00
Extreme Makeover (Jesus Edition)	$20.00
Fear Not!	$15.00
Gifts of the Spirit	$30.00
Golden Keys for a Successful Prayer Life	$20.00
Past, Present, & Future Ministry of Jesus Christ	$15.00
Preparing for a Year of Great Changes	$15.00
Qualifications for Supernatural Ministry	$20.00
Redeemed From the Curse!	$20.00
Relationships and How to Deal With Rejection	$15.00
School of Ministry: Five-Fold Ministry	$30.00
Spirit, Soul & Body	$20.00
School of Prayer	$10.00
The Influence, Person & Power of the Holy Spirit	$20.00
The Book of Revelation	$20.00
The Rapture	$10.00

Title of Amazing Music CDs	Price
The Work of the Apothecary Vol. I: Pure Worship	$15.00
All Yours	$15.00
The Work of the Apothecary Vol.II: Pure Worship	$15.00
The Work of the Apothecary Vol.III: Show Me Thy Face	$15.00
The Lord is a Man of War	$15.00
The Longing of My Heart	$15.00
Better Than Medicine	$15.00
Brand New Touch	$15.00
His Unfailing Love	$15.00
Just Give Me Jesus	$15.00
No Turning Back	$15.00
Precious Jesus	$15.00
Turning a Curse into a Blessing	$15.00
We Will Glorify	$15.00

To place an order and to view more selections of Pastor Jason Alvarez's Teachings and Music CDs:

Visit: www.theloveofjesus.org

Call: (973) 676-4200

Write: The Love of Jesus Family Church

448 Highland Avenue

Orange, NJ 07050

Made in the USA
Charleston, SC
29 September 2012